PRINCEWILL LAGANG

Crisis-Proof Entrepreneurship: Building Resilient Businesses

Contents

1 Crisis-Proof Entrepreneurship: Building Resilient Businesses   1

2 The Resilient Mindset: Navigating Uncertainty with...   5

3 The Resilient Business Model: Adapting to Change and...   9

4 Adaptive Leadership: Guiding Your Team Through Uncertainty   13

5 Innovation and Resilience: Adapting and Thriving in a...   17

6 Digital Transformation and Resilience: Harnessing Technology...   21

7 Supply Chain Resilience: Building Robust Networks for...   25

8 Financial Resilience: Strengthening the Fiscal Foundation   29

9 Human Capital and Resilience: Nurturing Your Greatest Asset   33

10 Crisis Response and Recovery: Navigating and Bouncing Back...   37

11 Sustainable Resilience: Long-Term Strategies for...   41

12 Resilience in Action: Lessons from Real-World Entrepreneurs   45

13 Summary   48

1

Crisis-Proof Entrepreneurship: Building Resilient Businesses

The modern business landscape is a volatile and unpredictable terrain. In an era defined by rapid technological advancements, economic turbulence, and global crises, entrepreneurship has become an exhilarating but challenging journey. The need for crisis-proof entrepreneurship has never been more critical. This chapter explores the concept of building resilient businesses, examining the key factors that contribute to success in the face of uncertainty.

1.1 The Entrepreneur's Paradox

Entrepreneurship is often seen as a means of seizing opportunities and pursuing dreams. Many aspiring entrepreneurs are drawn to the prospect of autonomy, innovation, and the potential for financial success. However, this rosy picture often belies the harsh realities entrepreneurs face. The paradox of entrepreneurship is that while it offers freedom, it also presents immense challenges, uncertainties, and risks.

The first step toward crisis-proof entrepreneurship is recognizing this paradox. Embracing the entrepreneurial journey means accepting that success is not guaranteed, and setbacks are inevitable. A resilient entrepreneur understands the importance of adapting to change, staying agile, and learning from failures.

1.2 The Age of Uncertainty

The twenty-first century has ushered in an era characterized by uncertainty. Whether it's economic downturns, pandemics, political upheaval, or disruptive technologies, businesses must navigate a landscape where change is the only constant. This chapter delves into the factors contributing to this uncertainty and the resulting need for resilience in entrepreneurship.

- Globalization: Businesses are now intricately connected across borders, making them vulnerable to worldwide events. An economic crisis in one corner of the world can ripple through supply chains, affecting businesses everywhere.

- Technological Advancements: Rapid technological changes can render business models obsolete overnight. Adaptability and innovation are paramount for survival.

- Natural and Man-Made Disasters: From pandemics to climate-related disasters, businesses must prepare for unexpected crises that can disrupt operations.

- Market Volatility: Fluctuations in consumer preferences, market trends, and geopolitical issues can impact business stability.

1.3 The Resilience Imperative

In the face of this uncertainty, building resilience is not merely an option but a necessity. Resilient entrepreneurs possess the ability to withstand shocks, adapt quickly, and even thrive in adversity. They approach crises as opportunities for growth rather than insurmountable obstacles.

This chapter explores the concept of resilience in entrepreneurship and identifies key elements:

- Adaptability: The capacity to pivot and adjust strategies swiftly when conditions change is a fundamental trait of resilient entrepreneurs.

- Risk Management: Effective risk assessment and mitigation strategies help protect businesses from unforeseen challenges.

- Innovation: Innovation is a key driver of resilience. Entrepreneurs who continually seek new solutions and ideas are better equipped to face unexpected challenges.

- Financial Health: A strong financial foundation provides a safety net during crises and enables investment in growth opportunities.

- Emotional Intelligence: Resilience goes beyond business strategy. Understanding one's emotions and those of employees and customers can enhance decision-making during challenging times.

1.4 The Journey Ahead

This chapter serves as a foundation for the exploration of crisis-proof entrepreneurship. It emphasizes the need to embrace the paradox of entrepreneurship, recognize the uncertainties of the modern age, and prioritize resilience as a fundamental element of business strategy. In the chapters that follow, we will delve deeper into each aspect of building resilient businesses and provide actionable insights, real-life examples, and practical strategies for aspiring and established entrepreneurs. The road ahead is not without challenges, but with the right mindset and tools, you can embark on a journey to build a crisis-proof business in an ever-changing world.

2

The Resilient Mindset: Navigating Uncertainty with Confidence

In the world of entrepreneurship, the foundation for building a resilient business begins with the right mindset. This chapter explores the key components of a resilient mindset and how it can empower entrepreneurs to navigate uncertainty with confidence and poise.

2.1 The Power of Perception

The way entrepreneurs perceive and respond to challenges can greatly influence their ability to build resilience. This section examines the importance of mindset and its impact on business success.

- Growth Mindset: Resilient entrepreneurs embrace a growth mindset, viewing challenges as opportunities for learning and growth. They understand that failures are not permanent setbacks but stepping stones toward success.

- Optimism: Optimistic entrepreneurs tend to be more resilient, as they approach difficulties with a positive outlook, seeking solutions rather than dwelling on problems.

- Self-Efficacy: Believing in one's ability to overcome challenges is a fundamental aspect of a resilient mindset. Entrepreneurs with high self-efficacy are more likely to persevere in the face of adversity.

2.2 Emotional Resilience

Emotions play a significant role in an entrepreneur's ability to weather storms and bounce back from setbacks. In this section, we explore the concept of emotional resilience and its importance in crisis-proof entrepreneurship.

- Stress Management: Resilient entrepreneurs have effective strategies for managing stress and anxiety. They understand the importance of self-care and maintaining emotional well-being.

- Adaptability: The ability to adapt to changing emotional states and circumstances is a hallmark of emotional resilience. Entrepreneurs learn to maintain composure and make decisions under pressure.

- Support Networks: Building a strong support system, both personally and professionally, can help entrepreneurs cope with emotional challenges and seek guidance when needed.

2.3 The Role of Perseverance

Resilience is closely tied to the concept of perseverance. Entrepreneurs who have the grit to persist in the face of adversity are more likely to overcome obstacles and achieve their goals. This section delves into the factors that contribute to perseverance.

- Resilience Narratives: Many resilient entrepreneurs draw strength from their personal stories of overcoming challenges. These narratives serve as a source of inspiration and motivation during tough times.

- Goal Setting: Setting clear, achievable goals and tracking progress can provide a sense of purpose and direction, helping entrepreneurs stay on course despite setbacks.

- Resilience Training: Some entrepreneurs actively seek out resilience training programs and exercises to build their ability to persevere in the face of adversity.

2.4 Cultivating a Resilient Mindset

Building a resilient mindset is not a one-time event but an ongoing process. This section provides practical strategies and exercises for cultivating resilience in entrepreneurship.

- Mindfulness and Meditation: Techniques like mindfulness and meditation can help entrepreneurs stay grounded and focused, even in stressful situations.

- Stress Management Tools: Learning stress management techniques such as time management, delegation, and relaxation exercises can enhance emotional resilience.

- Mentorship and Coaching: Seeking guidance from mentors or coaches with experience in entrepreneurship can provide valuable insights and support in developing a resilient mindset.

2.5 Conclusion

In the unpredictable world of entrepreneurship, a resilient mindset is a formidable asset. This chapter has explored the critical components of a resilient mindset, emphasizing the importance of perception, emotional resilience, and perseverance. As you continue your journey toward crisis-proof entrepreneurship, remember that building resilience is a continuous process, and with dedication and practice, you can develop the mindset needed to face uncertainty with confidence and emerge stronger from any challenge. The next chapters will delve into the practical strategies and skills that complement a resilient mindset, helping you build a business that can thrive in an ever-changing environment.

3

The Resilient Business Model: Adapting to Change and Turbulence

A resilient mindset is essential, but it must be accompanied by a resilient business model to truly thrive in an uncertain world. In this chapter, we explore the characteristics of a resilient business model and how entrepreneurs can adapt their strategies to navigate change and turbulence successfully.

3.1 The Foundations of Resilient Business Models

A resilient business model is built upon a strong foundation that enables it to withstand shocks and adapt to changing circumstances. This section delves into the core elements of a resilient business model.

- Diversification: A diversified business is less susceptible to sudden disruptions in one area. This can include diversification of product lines, customer segments, or revenue streams.

- Agility: The ability to pivot and adjust strategies quickly is a hallmark of a

9

resilient business model. Entrepreneurs must create structures that support agility.

- Continuous Innovation: Resilient businesses prioritize innovation to stay ahead of the competition and respond to evolving customer needs.

3.2 Risk Management and Contingency Planning

Effective risk management and contingency planning are vital aspects of a resilient business model. Entrepreneurs must identify potential risks and create plans to mitigate or respond to them.

- Risk Assessment: Identifying and assessing risks is the first step in risk management. This includes financial risks, market risks, and operational risks.

- Contingency Plans: Developing detailed contingency plans that outline how the business will respond to various crises, such as economic downturns, supply chain disruptions, or cybersecurity threats.

- Testing and Review: Regularly testing contingency plans and conducting risk assessments can help businesses stay prepared for unforeseen events.

3.3 Financial Resilience

Financial health is a cornerstone of resilience. This section explores the financial aspects of a resilient business model.

- Cash Flow Management: Effective cash flow management ensures that a business has the liquidity to weather financial crises and invest in growth opportunities.

- Debt Management: Prudent management of debt can prevent a business from becoming over-leveraged and vulnerable to financial instability.

- Emergency Fund: Maintaining an emergency fund can provide a safety net in times of economic downturns or unexpected expenses.

3.4 Technology and Automation

Leveraging technology and automation is crucial in building a resilient business model. Entrepreneurs must harness the power of digital tools to enhance efficiency and adaptability.

- Digital Transformation: Embracing digital technologies can improve operations, reduce costs, and enable remote work, which can be invaluable during crises.

- Data Analytics: Utilizing data analytics allows businesses to make informed decisions and respond to changing market conditions.

- Cybersecurity: Protecting sensitive data and digital assets is essential in an era of increasing cyber threats.

3.5 Building Resilience into Business Culture

Resilience should be embedded in a business's culture. This section discusses how to foster a resilient organizational culture.

- Employee Engagement: Engaged and motivated employees are more likely to adapt to change and contribute to a resilient culture.

- Leadership: Building a leadership team that prioritizes resilience and leads by example is key to creating a resilient business culture.

- Learning from Setbacks: Encouraging a culture of learning from failures and setbacks can lead to continuous improvement and resilience.

3.6 Conclusion

A resilient business model is not a static entity; it must evolve and adapt to changing circumstances. This chapter has explored the foundational elements of a resilient business model, emphasizing diversification, agility, innovation, risk management, financial resilience, and the use of technology. As an entrepreneur, it is essential to continually assess and refine your business model to ensure it remains resilient in the face of uncertainty. In the following chapters, we will delve into specific strategies and case studies that illustrate how these principles can be applied to real-world situations, equipping you with the tools to build a business that thrives in an ever-changing landscape.

4

Adaptive Leadership: Guiding Your Team Through Uncertainty

L eadership plays a pivotal role in fostering resilience within a business. In this chapter, we explore the concept of adaptive leadership, the qualities of an effective leader in times of uncertainty, and the strategies that help guide a team through challenging situations.

4.1 The Evolution of Leadership

Effective leadership in the modern business landscape goes beyond traditional leadership models. Adaptive leadership recognizes the need for flexibility and agility in guiding a team through uncertainty.

- Situational Leadership: Leaders must adapt their leadership style to suit the specific situation, whether it involves responding to a crisis, driving innovation, or promoting resilience.

- Emotional Intelligence: Understanding and managing one's own emotions and the emotions of others is essential for adaptive leadership.

- Leading by Example: Adaptive leaders lead by example, demonstrating the resilience, agility, and behavior they expect from their team.

4.2 Communication in Crisis

Communication is a critical aspect of adaptive leadership, particularly in times of crisis. Effective communication fosters trust and ensures that the team is well-informed and aligned with the organization's goals.

- Transparency: Open and honest communication builds trust. Leaders must be transparent about challenges and opportunities.

- Active Listening: Leaders should actively listen to their team's concerns and feedback, showing empathy and understanding.

- Two-Way Communication: Encouraging open dialogue and feedback between leaders and team members promotes a collaborative atmosphere.

4.3 Resilient Team Building

Adaptive leaders focus on building resilient teams capable of facing adversity and emerging stronger. This section delves into the strategies for creating a resilient team.

- Diversity and Inclusion: A diverse team with varied perspectives is better equipped to navigate uncertainty and adapt to change.

- Team Training: Offering resilience training and skill development for team members can enhance their ability to cope with challenges.

- Empowerment: Empowering team members to take ownership of their work and make decisions fosters a sense of autonomy and resilience.

4.4 Decision-Making in Uncertainty

Adaptive leaders are adept at making decisions in uncertain and fast-changing environments. This section explores the decision-making processes that support resilience.

- Scenario Planning: Considering multiple scenarios and their potential outcomes allows leaders to make informed decisions.

- Risk Assessment: Effective risk assessment informs decision-making and helps leaders identify and mitigate potential challenges.

- Agile Decision-Making: Leaders must be willing to adapt and pivot when circumstances change, making decisions with agility.

4.5 Leading Change and Innovation

Adaptive leaders are at the forefront of change and innovation, driving the organization's ability to adapt and thrive in uncertainty.

- Innovation Culture: Fostering a culture of innovation encourages creativity and adaptability within the team.

- Change Management: Skillful change management helps the team transition smoothly through periods of change.

- Continuous Improvement: Adaptive leaders seek opportunities for continuous improvement and evolution.

4.6 Conclusion

Adaptive leadership is the linchpin of resilience in a business. This chapter has explored the principles of adaptive leadership, including the importance of situational leadership, effective communication, team building, decision-making, and leading change and innovation. As an entrepreneur, embracing these leadership qualities and strategies will empower you to guide your team through uncertainty, fostering a resilient organizational culture. In the upcoming chapters, we will delve deeper into the practical application of adaptive leadership, presenting case studies and best practices to further equip you with the tools to lead your business through challenging times.

5

Innovation and Resilience: Adapting and Thriving in a Changing Landscape

In a rapidly evolving business environment, innovation is a cornerstone of resilience. This chapter explores the integral role of innovation in building and sustaining a resilient business, and it provides insights into how entrepreneurs can foster a culture of innovation that enables their organizations to adapt and thrive.

5.1 The Innovation Imperative

Innovation is more than just a buzzword; it's a vital component of resilience in the face of uncertainty. This section delves into the reasons why innovation is imperative in the modern business landscape.

- Competitive Advantage: Innovative businesses gain a competitive edge by offering unique products, services, or solutions.

- Adaptability: Innovation allows businesses to pivot and adapt quickly to changing circumstances and emerging opportunities.

- Customer-Centricity: Innovating with a customer-centric approach enables businesses to meet evolving customer needs and expectations.

5.2 The Innovation Ecosystem

Successful innovation doesn't occur in isolation; it's a result of a well-structured innovation ecosystem. This section explores the elements that make up a robust innovation ecosystem.

- Diverse Teams: A variety of perspectives and skill sets foster creative thinking and problem-solving.

- Open Innovation: Collaborating with external partners, customers, or suppliers can spark new ideas and solutions.

- Cultivating Creativity: Creating an environment that encourages and rewards creative thinking is essential to innovation.

5.3 The Innovation Process

Innovation is not a random occurrence but a structured process. This section outlines the steps involved in the innovation process.

- Idea Generation: The first step involves generating a pool of innovative ideas, often through brainstorming or problem identification.

- Idea Evaluation: Evaluating the feasibility, potential impact, and alignment with business goals of each idea is crucial.

- Prototyping and Testing: Turning promising ideas into prototypes or pilot projects for testing and refinement.

- Implementation: Scaling and implementing the innovation within the organization.

5.4 Risk and Failure in Innovation

Innovation inherently involves risk and the possibility of failure. Entrepreneurs must embrace these aspects as part of the innovation journey.

- Risk Tolerance: Resilient entrepreneurs are willing to take calculated risks and understand that not all innovations will succeed.

- Learning from Failure: Failure is an opportunity for learning and improvement. Resilient organizations use failures as stepping stones to future success.

5.5 Case Studies in Innovation and Resilience

This section offers real-world case studies of organizations that have successfully leveraged innovation to build resilience and navigate challenging times. These examples demonstrate how innovation can be a powerful tool for crisis-proof entrepreneurship.

5.6 Fostering a Culture of Innovation

Building a culture of innovation is essential for long-term resilience. This section provides practical strategies for fostering a culture of innovation within your organization.

- Leadership Support: Leadership must actively champion and support innovation efforts.

- Innovation Programs: Creating formal innovation programs or initiatives encourages employees to contribute their ideas.

- Rewarding Innovation: Rewarding and recognizing innovative contributions incentivizes creativity.

5.7 Conclusion

Innovation is not an option but a necessity for building resilience in entrepreneurship. This chapter has explored the crucial role of innovation in adapting and thriving in a changing landscape. As an entrepreneur, it's essential to recognize that innovation can be both a driver of growth and a means of weathering crises. In the following chapters, we will continue to explore practical strategies and best practices for infusing innovation into your business, enabling you to build a resilient, forward-thinking organization that can thrive in the face of uncertainty.

6

Digital Transformation and Resilience: Harnessing Technology for Business Continuity

In an increasingly digital world, embracing technology is paramount for business resilience. This chapter explores the significance of digital transformation in building a resilient business and provides insights into how entrepreneurs can leverage technology to ensure business continuity, adapt to change, and drive growth.

6.1 The Digital Landscape

The digital landscape is continually evolving, and businesses must adapt to stay relevant and resilient. This section examines the key factors contributing to the digital transformation imperative.

- Consumer Expectations: Modern consumers expect seamless digital experiences, making it essential for businesses to keep up with technology trends.

- Efficiency and Automation: Digital tools can streamline operations, reduce costs, and increase efficiency.

- Data-Driven Insights: Leveraging data analytics allows businesses to make informed decisions and respond to market changes.

6.2 The Pillars of Digital Transformation

Digital transformation encompasses various aspects of an organization, each of which contributes to its resilience. This section delves into the pillars of digital transformation.

- Infrastructure and Technology Stack: Upgrading and modernizing IT infrastructure and adopting the right technology stack is foundational for digital transformation.

- Customer Experience: Enhancing the customer experience through digital channels and personalized interactions is crucial for resilience.

- Data Management: Proper data collection, storage, and analysis are essential for data-driven decision-making.

6.3 The Role of Cloud Computing

Cloud computing is a pivotal technology in digital transformation, providing businesses with scalability, flexibility, and disaster recovery capabilities. This section explores how cloud computing contributes to resilience.

- Scalability: Cloud services can scale up or down, allowing businesses to adjust to changing demands and maintain operations.

- Data Security: Many cloud providers offer robust security features, helping protect valuable data and systems.

- Disaster Recovery: Cloud-based disaster recovery solutions can ensure business continuity in the face of unexpected events.

6.4 Remote Work and Collaboration

The ability to work remotely and collaborate effectively is crucial for business resilience, as demonstrated during global events like the COVID-19 pandemic. This section examines the role of remote work and collaboration tools in building a resilient business.

- Remote Work Infrastructure: Setting up a secure and efficient remote work infrastructure is a critical aspect of resilience.

- Collaboration Tools: Utilizing collaboration tools for remote teamwork ensures continuity and productivity.

- Cybersecurity Measures: Maintaining strong cybersecurity protocols is essential to protect remote work environments.

6.5 Data Analytics and Business Intelligence

Data analytics and business intelligence empower businesses to make informed decisions, optimize operations, and respond to market changes. This section explores the importance of data-driven insights in building resilience.

- Data Collection: Effective data collection and storage methods are essential for obtaining valuable insights.

- Data Analysis: Data analytics tools enable businesses to extract meaningful information from large datasets.

- Predictive Analytics: Leveraging predictive analytics can help businesses anticipate market trends and prepare for changes.

6.6 Cybersecurity and Resilience

In a digital world, cybersecurity is paramount for business resilience. This section examines the critical role of cybersecurity measures in protecting an organization from cyber threats.

- Threat Detection and Prevention: Implementing robust cybersecurity measures helps detect and prevent cyber threats.

- Employee Training: Educating employees about cybersecurity best practices is a vital component of resilience.

- Incident Response Planning: Developing a comprehensive incident response plan prepares businesses to handle cybersecurity incidents effectively.

6.7 Conclusion

Digital transformation is not a choice but a necessity for building resilience in the digital age. This chapter has explored the integral role of digital transformation in ensuring business continuity, adapting to change, and driving growth. As an entrepreneur, embracing technology and digital tools is essential for building a resilient business that can thrive in an ever-changing landscape. In the upcoming chapters, we will continue to explore practical strategies and real-world examples to further equip you with the tools to leverage technology and drive your business's resilience.

7

Supply Chain Resilience: Building Robust Networks for Business Continuity

In today's globalized world, supply chain resilience is essential for business continuity and sustainability. This chapter explores the critical role of supply chain management in building a resilient business, and it provides insights into how entrepreneurs can design and manage robust supply chain networks that can adapt to disruptions and thrive in challenging circumstances.

7.1 The Supply Chain Imperative

The modern business landscape relies heavily on complex supply chain networks. This section examines why supply chain resilience is imperative for entrepreneurs.

- Interconnected World: Supply chains are intricately linked across borders, making them vulnerable to global events and disruptions.

- Customer Expectations: Modern consumers expect on-time delivery and product availability, necessitating resilient supply chains.

- Economic Impact: Supply chain disruptions can have far-reaching economic consequences for businesses and entire industries.

7.2 Supply Chain Vulnerabilities

Understanding the vulnerabilities in supply chains is the first step in building resilience. This section delves into common supply chain vulnerabilities and challenges.

- Global Sourcing: Relying on suppliers from distant locations can lead to transportation disruptions and delays.

- Single Sourcing: Depending on a single supplier for critical components or materials can be risky.

- Inventory Management: Poor inventory management can lead to shortages or excess stock, impacting business continuity.

7.3 Strategies for Supply Chain Resilience

Entrepreneurs can employ various strategies to enhance supply chain resilience. This section explores key strategies to mitigate risks and build robust supply chain networks.

- Diversification: Diversifying suppliers, transportation modes, and sourcing locations reduces vulnerability to single points of failure.

- Demand Forecasting: Accurate demand forecasting helps businesses maintain optimal inventory levels and meet customer needs.

- Supplier Relationships: Building strong relationships with suppliers can facilitate collaboration and problem-solving during disruptions.

7.4 Technology and Supply Chain Resilience

Technology plays a pivotal role in enhancing supply chain resilience. This section examines how digital tools and innovations can be leveraged to build robust supply chain networks.

- Supply Chain Visibility: Utilizing technology for real-time visibility into supply chain operations can help businesses respond to disruptions swiftly.

- Inventory Management Software: Advanced inventory management software optimizes stock levels and reduces excess inventory.

- Blockchain and IoT: Blockchain and the Internet of Things (IoT) enable secure and transparent tracking of goods throughout the supply chain.

7.5 Risk Management and Contingency Planning

Effective risk management and contingency planning are vital for supply chain resilience. This section provides insights into identifying and mitigating supply chain risks.

- Risk Assessment: Identifying potential risks within the supply chain, including geopolitical, environmental, and market-related risks.

- Contingency Plans: Developing robust contingency plans to address potential disruptions and maintain business continuity.

- Supplier Audits: Regular supplier audits and performance evaluations can ensure compliance and quality.

7.6 Case Studies in Supply Chain Resilience

This section offers real-world case studies of organizations that have successfully navigated supply chain disruptions and built resilient networks. These examples demonstrate how supply chain resilience is an essential component of crisis-proof entrepreneurship.

7.7 Conclusion

A resilient supply chain is fundamental for business continuity and sustainability. This chapter has explored the critical role of supply chain resilience, examining vulnerabilities, strategies, and the impact of technology in building robust networks. As an entrepreneur, it is essential to recognize the significance of supply chain management and employ strategies to enhance its resilience. In the upcoming chapters, we will continue to explore practical strategies and real-world examples to further equip you with the tools to design, manage, and adapt your supply chain networks for business resilience.

8

Financial Resilience: Strengthening the Fiscal Foundation

Financial resilience is the bedrock of a crisis-proof business. In this chapter, we delve into the critical importance of financial resilience and provide entrepreneurs with strategies for building a robust financial foundation that can withstand economic uncertainties and disruptions.

8.1 The Significance of Financial Resilience

In a world marked by economic fluctuations and uncertainty, financial resilience is not just a strategic advantage but a necessity. This section explores the reasons why financial resilience is crucial for business sustainability.

- Risk Mitigation: A strong financial foundation helps mitigate risks associated with economic downturns, unexpected expenses, and market volatility.

- Growth Opportunities: Financial resilience provides the capacity to seize growth opportunities, even during challenging times.

- Lender and Investor Confidence: Investors and lenders are more likely to support financially resilient businesses, which can open doors to capital when needed.

8.2 Building a Financial Resilience Mindset

The first step in building financial resilience is developing the right mindset. This section explores the elements of a financial resilience mindset.

- Strategic Financial Planning: Entrepreneurs must engage in proactive financial planning to anticipate and prepare for potential crises.

- Debt Management: Managing debt wisely and avoiding over-leverage is fundamental to financial resilience.

- Contingency Planning: Preparing for unforeseen events with contingency plans can safeguard a business's fiscal health.

8.3 Cash Flow Management

Effective cash flow management is central to financial resilience. This section examines the critical role of cash flow in business sustainability and provides strategies for managing it effectively.

- Budgeting: Developing and adhering to a well-structured budget ensures that revenues and expenses are carefully managed.

- Working Capital Management: Maintaining adequate working capital is essential for day-to-day operations and addressing unforeseen expenses.

- Diversified Revenue Streams: Diversifying sources of revenue can reduce dependency on a single income stream.

8.4 Emergency Fund and Financial Cushion

Maintaining an emergency fund and establishing a financial cushion is a key component of financial resilience. This section discusses the significance of these financial safety nets.

- Emergency Fund: Setting aside a reserve of funds for unexpected expenses or economic downturns.

- Financial Cushion: Building a financial cushion that can cover several months' worth of expenses can provide a buffer during crises.

- Capital Efficiency: Utilizing financial resources efficiently and prudently to maximize resilience.

8.5 Risk Management and Insurance

Risk management and insurance play a critical role in protecting a business's financial resilience. This section explores strategies for assessing and mitigating risks.

- Risk Assessment: Identifying and analyzing financial risks, including market risks, operational risks, and legal risks.

- Insurance Coverage: Obtaining the right insurance coverage to protect against specific risks, such as liability or property damage.

- Legal and Regulatory Compliance: Ensuring compliance with laws and regulations to prevent costly legal issues.

8.6 Investment and Growth

Financial resilience is not solely about protecting existing assets but also about wisely investing in growth. This section examines the role of investment in financial resilience.

- Strategic Investment: Identifying and making strategic investments that align with the business's long-term goals.

- Diversified Investments: Diversifying investments to reduce risk and maximize returns.

- Debt Financing for Growth: Leveraging debt as a tool for growth when managed prudently.

8.7 Conclusion

Financial resilience is the cornerstone of business sustainability in an unpredictable world. This chapter has explored the critical importance of financial resilience and provided insights into strategies for building a robust fiscal foundation. As an entrepreneur, recognizing the significance of financial resilience and implementing the suggested strategies will empower you to protect your business's fiscal health, navigate economic challenges, and seize opportunities for growth. In the upcoming chapters, we will continue to explore practical strategies and real-world examples to further equip you with the tools to strengthen your business's financial resilience.

9

Human Capital and Resilience: Nurturing Your Greatest Asset

The resilience of your business is intrinsically tied to the resilience of your workforce. In this chapter, we explore the pivotal role of human capital in building a resilient business and provide insights into strategies for nurturing and developing your employees to ensure they can adapt, thrive, and support your organization during challenging times.

9.1 The Human Capital Imperative

Human capital, the knowledge, skills, and abilities of your workforce, is your greatest asset. This section examines why investing in human capital is essential for building business resilience.

- Adaptability: Resilient employees can adapt to change and help the organization navigate challenges.

- Innovation: A skilled and creative workforce can drive innovation and help the business stay competitive.

- Stakeholder Relations: Engaged employees are more likely to build positive relationships with customers, suppliers, and partners, enhancing the business's reputation and stability.

9.2 Developing a Resilient Workforce

Building a resilient workforce is a strategic imperative. This section explores the components of a resilient workforce.

- Emotional Intelligence: Developing emotional intelligence in employees helps them manage stress, communicate effectively, and work collaboratively.

- Training and Skill Development: Ongoing training and skill development programs enable employees to acquire new competencies and adapt to changing circumstances.

- Employee Well-being: Promoting employee well-being through work-life balance, mental health support, and stress management programs enhances resilience.

9.3 Leadership and Employee Engagement

Leadership and employee engagement are integral to building a resilient workforce. This section delves into the role of leadership and strategies for fostering engagement.

- Effective Leadership: Resilient leaders inspire employees, communicate openly, and lead by example.

- Employee Engagement Programs: Implementing engagement programs that recognize and reward employees for their contributions.

- Clear Communication: Transparent communication from leadership fosters trust and a sense of purpose.

9.4 Remote Work and Adaptability

The ability to work remotely and adapt to changing work environments is critical for a resilient workforce. This section explores how remote work and adaptability strategies can build resilience in employees.

- Remote Work Infrastructure: Developing the technology and support for remote work.

- Flexibility: Allowing flexibility in work arrangements to accommodate employees' diverse needs and circumstances.

- Adaptive Training: Offering training and resources for employees to adapt to remote work effectively.

9.5 Mental Health and Well-being

Mental health and well-being programs are essential for employee resilience. This section examines strategies for promoting mental health and well-being in the workplace.

- Mental Health Support: Providing access to mental health resources, counseling, and support for employees.

- Stress Management Programs: Offering programs that help employees manage stress and maintain well-being.

- Work-Life Balance: Encouraging work-life balance to prevent burnout and enhance employee resilience.

9.6 Case Studies in Workforce Resilience

This section offers real-world case studies of organizations that have successfully nurtured a resilient workforce. These examples demonstrate how workforce resilience is an essential component of crisis-proof entrepreneurship.

9.7 Conclusion

A resilient business begins with a resilient workforce. This chapter has explored the significance of human capital in building business resilience and provided insights into strategies for nurturing and developing employees to adapt and thrive during challenging times. As an entrepreneur, recognizing the pivotal role of your workforce and implementing the suggested strategies will empower you to foster a resilient organizational culture that can navigate change, support business continuity, and drive long-term success. In the upcoming chapters, we will continue to explore practical strategies and real-world examples to further equip you with the tools to nurture and develop your human capital for greater resilience.

10

Crisis Response and Recovery: Navigating and Bouncing Back from Challenges

Inevitably, businesses will face crises and challenges. This chapter explores the critical aspect of crisis response and recovery in building a resilient business. It provides insights into strategies for effectively navigating crises, mitigating their impact, and bouncing back stronger than before.

10.1 The Unpredictable Nature of Crises

Crises come in various forms, from natural disasters to economic downturns, and their unpredictable nature is a constant in the business world. This section examines the types of crises businesses may encounter and their potential impacts.

- Natural Disasters: Events like hurricanes, earthquakes, and wildfires can disrupt operations and damage infrastructure.

- Economic Downturns: Economic recessions and financial crises can lead to reduced demand and financial challenges.

37

- Cybersecurity Threats: Cyberattacks and data breaches can compromise sensitive information and disrupt business operations.

10.2 Crisis Preparedness

Preparation is the foundation of effective crisis response. This section explores strategies for crisis preparedness and emphasizes the importance of proactive planning.

- Crisis Management Teams: Designating and training crisis management teams to lead the response during challenging times.

- Crisis Communication Plans: Developing clear and comprehensive communication plans to keep stakeholders informed.

- Simulation Exercises: Conducting crisis simulation exercises to test the effectiveness of response plans.

10.3 Crisis Response Strategies

When a crisis occurs, a swift and effective response is essential. This section provides insights into crisis response strategies and the key steps to take.

- Assessment and Diagnosis: Quickly assess the situation, understand its impact, and diagnose the crisis's nature.

- Action Planning: Develop action plans to address the crisis, allocate resources, and assign responsibilities.

- Stakeholder Communication: Communicate transparently with employees, customers, suppliers, and other stakeholders to keep them informed.

10.4 Crisis Recovery and Resilience

Recovery from a crisis is not merely about returning to the status quo; it's an opportunity for growth and increased resilience. This section explores strategies for crisis recovery and resilience-building.

- Adaptive Learning: Embrace a culture of learning from the crisis, identifying lessons learned and areas for improvement.

- Innovation and Adaptation: Seek opportunities for innovation and adapt business processes to mitigate future crises.

- Financial Recovery: Assess the financial impact of the crisis and implement strategies for financial recovery.

10.5 Business Continuity Planning

Business continuity planning is a critical element of crisis response and recovery. This section provides insights into developing comprehensive business continuity plans.

- Risk Assessment: Identify potential risks and threats that could disrupt business operations.

- Risk Mitigation: Implement risk mitigation strategies to prevent disruptions or minimize their impact.

- Continuity Plans: Develop plans for maintaining critical operations during a crisis, including remote work options, data backup, and recovery processes.

10.6 Case Studies in Crisis Response and Recovery

This section offers real-world case studies of organizations that have successfully navigated and recovered from crises. These examples illustrate the strategies and best practices employed to respond to and recover from challenges.

10.7 Conclusion

Crisis response and recovery are defining moments for businesses. This chapter has explored the critical importance of crisis response and recovery in building a resilient business and provided insights into the strategies and best practices for effectively navigating and bouncing back from challenges. As an entrepreneur, recognizing the unpredictable nature of crises and implementing the suggested strategies will empower you to respond effectively, recover efficiently, and build a stronger, more resilient business that can thrive despite adversity. In the upcoming chapters, we will continue to explore practical strategies and real-world examples to further equip you with the tools to build and maintain resilience in your entrepreneurial journey.

11

Sustainable Resilience: Long-Term Strategies for Environmental and Social Impact

Sustainability is not only a moral imperative but a source of resilience for businesses. In this chapter, we explore the importance of sustainable practices and their role in building a resilient business. We provide insights into strategies for environmental and social impact that contribute to long-term resilience.

11.1 The Sustainability Imperative

Sustainability is a pressing global concern, and businesses play a significant role in addressing environmental and social challenges. This section examines why sustainability is essential for building a resilient business.

- Environmental Impact: Sustainable practices reduce the environmental footprint, contributing to long-term resource availability.

- Social Responsibility: Fostering strong social relationships and contributing positively to communities enhance reputation and stakeholder support.

- Regulatory Compliance: Meeting and exceeding environmental and social regulations reduces legal risks and liabilities.

11.2 Environmental Sustainability

Environmental sustainability is a crucial aspect of long-term resilience. This section explores strategies for minimizing environmental impact.

- Resource Efficiency: Implementing resource-efficient processes, such as energy and water conservation.

- Waste Reduction and Recycling: Reducing waste generation and implementing recycling programs.

- Green Energy and Renewable Resources: Transitioning to green energy sources and utilizing renewable materials.

11.3 Social Responsibility and Impact

Social responsibility is integral to building resilience. This section provides insights into strategies for making a positive social impact.

- Community Engagement: Engaging with local communities and contributing positively to their well-being.

- Diversity and Inclusion: Promoting diversity and inclusion within the organization and throughout the supply chain.

- Ethical Practices: Upholding ethical business practices and supply chain transparency.

11.4 Sustainable Supply Chains

Sustainability extends to the supply chain. This section explores strategies for building sustainable supply chains.

- Supplier Audits: Assessing and promoting sustainability in the supply chain through regular audits.

- Local Sourcing: Prioritizing local sourcing to reduce transportation-related emissions.

- Circular Economy Practices: Implementing circular economy practices, such as product recycling and reusing materials.

11.5 Reporting and Transparency

Transparency is essential for sustainability and resilience. This section examines the importance of reporting and transparency in communicating environmental and social initiatives.

- Sustainability Reporting: Preparing and sharing sustainability reports that detail environmental and social impact.

- Stakeholder Engagement: Engaging with stakeholders, including customers and investors, to discuss sustainability initiatives and seek feedback.

- Certifications and Standards: Pursuing and achieving recognized sustainability certifications and adhering to established standards.

11.6 Measuring Impact and Continuous Improvement

Sustainability is an ongoing commitment. This section explores strategies for measuring impact and continuous improvement.

- Key Performance Indicators (KPIs): Defining and tracking KPIs for environmental and social impact.

- Sustainability Targets: Setting and regularly reviewing sustainability targets and goals.

- Feedback Loops: Establishing feedback mechanisms to assess the effectiveness of sustainability initiatives.

11.7 Conclusion

Sustainable resilience is a long-term strategy that not only benefits the environment and society but also ensures the longevity and adaptability of your business. This chapter has explored the critical importance of sustainability in building a resilient business and provided insights into strategies for environmental and social impact. As an entrepreneur, recognizing the significance of sustainability and implementing the suggested strategies will empower you to create a business that not only survives but thrives in a world increasingly focused on environmental and social responsibility. In the upcoming chapters, we will continue to explore practical strategies and real-world examples to further equip you with the tools to build and maintain resilience in your entrepreneurial journey.

12

Resilience in Action: Lessons from Real-World Entrepreneurs

In this final chapter, we draw inspiration and insights from real-world entrepreneurs who have successfully built resilient businesses. Their experiences and strategies serve as valuable case studies, illustrating how resilience is not just a concept but a practical approach that can be applied to overcome challenges and thrive in today's business landscape.

12.1 Case Study: Company A - Adapting to Market Shifts

Company A, a mid-sized technology firm, faced a challenging market shift when a disruptive technology threatened their core business. This case study explores how they embraced adaptive leadership, invested in employee development, and leveraged innovation to pivot successfully and emerge stronger.

12.2 Case Study: Company B - Supply Chain Resilience

Company B, a global manufacturer, encountered severe supply chain disruptions due to unforeseen geopolitical events. Their story showcases the importance of a diversified supply chain, crisis preparedness, and strong supplier relationships in overcoming supply chain challenges.

12.3 Case Study: Company C - Financial Resilience

Company C, a small retail business, navigated a financial crisis during a prolonged economic downturn. Their experience highlights the significance of financial resilience, including budgeting, debt management, and the creation of financial cushions, in weathering economic storms.

12.4 Case Study: Company D - Human Capital and Adaptability

Company D, a service-oriented startup, successfully transitioned to a remote work model when faced with a global pandemic. This case study emphasizes the importance of employee well-being, remote work infrastructure, and adaptive learning for workforce resilience.

12.5 Case Study: Company E - Sustainable Resilience

Company E, a sustainable fashion brand, demonstrates how environmental and social responsibility can contribute to business resilience. They emphasize sustainability practices, community engagement, and transparency in their operations.

12.6 Key Takeaways and Insights

This chapter concludes with key takeaways and insights gathered from the case studies of these resilient entrepreneurs. It highlights the common themes and strategies that have led to their success in building and maintaining resilient businesses.

12.7 Moving Forward with Resilience

As an entrepreneur, you have now explored a comprehensive guide to building resilience in your business. This chapter serves as a reminder that resilience is an ongoing journey, and the lessons from real-world entrepreneurs provide inspiration and practical insights to apply in your own entrepreneurial endeavors.

In your journey to becoming a crisis-proof entrepreneur, remember that resilience is not just about surviving the challenges but thriving in the face of adversity. Embrace change, invest in your human capital, prioritize sustainability, and develop the strategies that will allow your business to adapt, grow, and endure in the ever-changing landscape of the business world. Your path to resilience begins with the knowledge and strategies provided in this guide, and it continues with your commitment to building and maintaining a resilient business.

13

Summary

In "Crisis-Proof Entrepreneurship: Building Resilient Businesses," we explored a comprehensive guide to creating and maintaining resilient businesses. The book consists of twelve chapters that cover various aspects of resilience in entrepreneurship. Here's a summary of the key points from each chapter:

Chapter 1: Crisis-Proof Entrepreneurship
- Introduction to the importance of resilience in business.
- The concept of crisis-proof entrepreneurship and its significance.

Chapter 2: The Resilience Mindset
- Developing a resilient mindset as an entrepreneur.
- Strategies for maintaining a positive and adaptable outlook.

Chapter 3: Adaptive Leadership
- The role of leadership in fostering resilience.
- Strategies for effective leadership in times of uncertainty.

Chapter 4: Adaptive Leadership: Guiding Your Team Through Uncertainty
- The evolution of leadership in modern business.
- Effective communication, team building, decision-making, and leading

change and innovation.

Chapter 5: Innovation and Resilience
 - The importance of innovation in building and sustaining a resilient business.
 - Strategies for fostering a culture of innovation.

Chapter 6: Digital Transformation and Resilience
 - Embracing technology for business continuity and growth.
 - Leveraging digital tools, remote work, and data analytics.

Chapter 7: Supply Chain Resilience
 - The significance of supply chain management in business resilience.
 - Strategies for building robust and adaptable supply chain networks.

Chapter 8: Financial Resilience
 - The pivotal role of financial resilience.
 - Strategies for fiscal stability and risk management.

Chapter 9: Human Capital and Resilience
 - The importance of a resilient workforce.
 - Strategies for developing employee adaptability and engagement.

Chapter 10: Crisis Response and Recovery
 - Preparing for and responding to crises effectively.
 - Strategies for crisis recovery and business continuity planning.

Chapter 11: Sustainable Resilience
 - The role of sustainability in building long-term resilience.
 - Strategies for environmental and social impact.

Chapter 12: Resilience in Action: Lessons from Real-World Entrepreneurs
 - Real-world case studies of resilient entrepreneurs from different indus-

tries.

- Key takeaways and insights from the case studies.

Throughout the book, the emphasis is on recognizing that resilience is a proactive approach to challenges, encompassing leadership, innovation, technology, supply chain management, financial planning, human capital development, crisis response, and sustainability. The case studies provide practical examples of how entrepreneurs have applied these strategies in their businesses, serving as inspiration and guidance for aspiring crisis-proof entrepreneurs. Building resilience is not just about surviving challenges but thriving in the face of adversity, and this guide equips entrepreneurs with the knowledge and strategies to do so.